First hundred words in Chinese

Heather Amery

Illustrated by Stephen Cartwright

Translation and pronunciation guide by
Quarto Translations

Designed by Mike Olley and Jan McCafferty

 There is a little yellow duck to find in every picture.

客厅 *kè tīng* The living room

爸爸
bà ba Daddy

妈妈
mā ma Mommy

男孩
nán hái boy

2

女孩　　　　　　　婴儿　　　　　　　狗　　　　　　　猫

nǚ hái　girl　　　　*yīng ér*　baby　　　　*gǒu*　dog　　　　*māo*　cat

衣服　*yī fu*　Clothes

鞋 内裤 套头衫

xié　shoes　　*nèi kù*　underwear　　*tào tóu shān*　sweater

汗衫	裤子	T恤	短袜
àn shān undershirt	*kù zi* pants	*tee shoo* t-shirt	*duǎn wà* socks

早餐 *zǎo cān* Breakfast

面包

miàn bāo　bread

牛奶

niú nǎi　milk

鸡蛋

jī dàn　eggs

6

苹果   橙子   香蕉

píng guǒ   apple   *chéng zi*   orange   *xiāng jiāo*   banana

厨房 *chú fáng*   The kitchen

桌子

zhuō zi   table

椅子

yǐ zi   chair

盘子

pán zi   plate

刀子
dāo zi   knife

餐叉
cān chā   fork

勺子
sháo zi   spoon

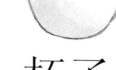
杯子
bēi zi   cup

玩具 *wán jù* Toys

马

mǎ horse

羊

yáng sheep

母牛

mǔ niú cow

母鸡
mǔ jī hen

猪
zhū pig

火车
huǒ chē train

积木
jī mù blocks

拜访 *bài fǎng* On a visit

奶奶
nǎi nai Grandma

爷爷
yé ye Grandpa

拖鞋
tuō xié slippers

外套
wài tào coat

连衣裙
lián yī qún dress

帽子
mào zi hat

公园 *gōng yuán* The park

树
shù tree

花
huā flower

秋千
qiū qiān swings

球
qiú ball

14

滑梯
huá tī slide

靴子
xuē zi boots

鸟
niǎo bird

船
chuán boat

街道　*jiē dào*　The street

汽车
qì chē　car

自行车
zì xíng chē　bicycle

飞机
fēi jī　airplane

卡车

kǎ chē　truck

公共汽车

gōng gòng qì chē　bus

房子

fáng zi　house

聚会 *jù huì* The party

气球

qì qiú balloon

蛋糕

dàn gāo cake

时钟

shí zhōng clock

冰淇淋　　　　鱼　　　　饼干　　　　糖果

īng qí lín　ice cream　*yú*　fish　*bǐng gān*　cookies　*táng guǒ*　candy

游泳池

yóu yǒng chí   The swimming pool

手臂
shǒu bì   arm

手
shǒu   hand

腿
tuǐ   leg

脚

jiǎo feet

脚趾

jiǎo zhǐ toes

头

tóu head

屁股

pì gu bottom

更衣室 gēng yī shì The changing room

嘴
zuǐ mouth

眼睛
yǎn jing eyes

耳朵
ěr duo ears

 鼻子
bí zi nose

 头发
tóu fa hair

 梳子
shū zi comb

 刷子
shuā zi brush

23

商店 *shāng diàn* The store

红色
hóng sè red

蓝色
lán sè blue

绿色
lǜ sè green

24

黄色
huáng sè   yellow

粉红色
fěn hóng sè   pink

白色
bái sè   white

黑色
hēi sè   black

浴室　*yù shì*　The bathroom

肥皂

féi zào　soap

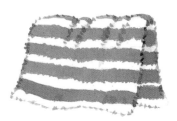

毛巾

máo jīn　towel

抽水马桶

chōu shuǐ mǎ tǒng　toile

浴缸
yù gāng bathtub

肚子
dù zi tummy

鸭子
yā zi duck

卧室 *wò shì* The bedroom

床
chuáng bed

灯
dēng light

窗户
chuāng hu window

28

门
mén door

书
shū book

洋娃娃
yáng wá wa doll

泰迪熊
tài dí xióng
teddy bear

29

Match the words to the pictures

书
shū

靴子
xuē zi

火车
huǒ chē

洋娃娃
yáng wá wa

汗衫
hàn shān

鱼
yú

球
qiú

蛋糕
dàn gāo

母牛
mǔ niú

套头衫
tào tóu shān

时钟
shí zhōng

香蕉
xiāng jiāo

餐叉
cān chā

鸭子
yā zi

窗户
chuāng hu

猫
māo

狗
gǒu

牛奶
niú nǎi

短袜
duǎn wà

桌子
zhuō zi

苹果
píng guǒ

帽子
mào zi

灯
dēng

猪
zhū

冰淇淋
bīng qí lín

刀子
dāo zi

泰迪熊
tài dí xióng

汽车
qì chē

橙子
chéng zi

鸡蛋
jī dàn

数字　*shù zi*　Numbers

1 一
yī　one

2 二
èr　two

3 三
sān　three

4 四
sì　four

5 五
wǔ　five

1 一
yī
one

2 二
èr
two

3 三
sān
three

4 四
sì
four

5 五
wǔ
five

Reading *pinyin*

Almost all Chinese-English dictionaries, as well as this book, use the pronunciation system called *pinyin*. Read the *pinyin* words as if you were reading English, but:

	has a harsher sound, like the Scottish *ch* in *loch*
	sounds like the *ch* in *cheer*
	sounds like the *s* in *see*
	sounds like the *ts* in *cats*
	sounds like the *ds* in *heads*

The next four are said with your tongue rolled back:

ch	sounds like the *ch* in *cheer*
sh	sounds like the *sh* in *shy*
zh	sounds like the *dge* in *fudge*
r	sounds like the *r* in *ring*

a	sounds like the *a* in *car*
an	sounds like the *an* in *can't*
e	sounds like the *e* in *the* or *mother*
en	sounds like the *en* in *shaken*
i	can sound like the *ee* in *seen*, or like the *i* in *shirt*, but
in	sounds like the *in* in *fin*
o	sounds like the *o* in *more*, and
ong	sounds like the *ung* in *sung*, but longer, more like *soong*
u	sounds like the *oo* in *too*
ü	for this sound, round your lips to say *oo*, then try saying *ee*

In Mandarin Chinese there are four tones, which means that the vowel sounds *a e i o u*, or groups of vowels, can be said in different ways:
1. The first tone is high and level.
   In *pinyin* it is written ˉ, as in *huā* (flower)
2. The second tone starts lower and then rises.
   It is written ´, as in *mén* (door)
3. The third tone starts in the middle, falls then rises.
   It is written ˇ, as in *wǔ* (five)
4. The fourth tone starts high and then falls.
   It is written `, as in *shù* (tree)

Some vowel sounds, often in the second part of a word, are said without a particular tone and so are written without a tone mark. It is important to use the right tone because the same word can have very different meanings when said with different tones – for example, *mā* means "mother" but *mǎ* means "horse."

Word list

This list shows all the words in this book in the alphabetical order of the English words. Next are the Chinese words written in Chinese characters, then the *pinyin* guide to show you how to say them.

English	Chinese	Pinyin
airplane	飞机	*fēi jī*
apple	苹果	*píng guǒ*
arm	手臂	*shǒu bì*
baby	婴儿	*yīng ér*
ball	球	*qiú*
balloon	气球	*qì qiú*
banana	香蕉	*xiāng jiāo*
bathroom	浴室	*yù shì*
bathtub	浴缸	*yù gāng*
bed	床	*chuáng*
bedroom	卧室	*wò shì*
bicycle	自行车	*zì xíng chē*
bird	鸟	*niǎo*
black	黑色	*hēi sè*
blocks	积木	*jī mù*
blue	蓝色	*lán sè*
boat	船	*chuán*
book	书	*shū*
boots	靴子	*xuē zi*
bottom	屁股	*pì gu*
boy	男孩	*nán hái*
bread	面包	*miàn bāo*
breakfast	早餐	*zǎo cān*
brush	刷子	*shuā zi*
bus	公共汽车	*gōng gòng qì chē*
cake	蛋糕	*dàn gāo*
candy	糖果	*táng guǒ*
car	汽车	*qì chē*
cat	猫	*māo*
chair	椅子	*yǐ zi*

English	Chinese	Pinyin
changing room	更衣室	*gēng yī shì*
clock	时钟	*shí zhōng*
clothes	衣服	*yī fu*
coat	外套	*wài tào*
comb	梳子	*shū zi*
cookies	饼干	*bǐng gān*
cow	母牛	*mǔ niú*
cup	杯子	*bēi zi*
Daddy	爸爸	*bà ba*
dog	狗	*gǒu*
doll	洋娃娃	*yáng wá wa*
door	门	*mén*
dress	连衣裙	*lián yī qún*
duck	鸭子	*yā zi*
ears	耳朵	*ěr duo*
egg / eggs	鸡蛋	*jī dàn*
eyes	眼睛	*yǎn jing*
feet	脚	*jiǎo*
fish	鱼	*yú*
five	五	*wǔ*
flower	花	*huā*
fork	餐叉	*cān chā*
four	四	*sì*
girl	女孩	*nǚ hái*
Grandma	奶奶	*nǎi nai*
(father's mother)	奶奶	*nǎi nai*
(mother's mother)	外婆	*wài pó*
Grandpa	爷爷	*yé ye*
(father's father)	爷爷	*yé ye*
(mother's father)	外公	*wài gōng*